Just Grandpa

Written by **Will and Le Anne Barber**
Illustrated by **Martha Klymkiw**

Celebration Press
An Imprint of Pearson Learning

MW00571562

I milk the cows.
Just like Grandpa.

I feed the chickens.

Just like Grandpa.

I sweep the barn.
Just like Grandpa.

I paint the fence.

Just like Grandpa.

I pick the apples.

Just like Grandpa.

I carry the wood.

Just like Grandpa.

I take a nap.

Just like Grandpa.